# ACT UP!
## THE WAR AGAINST HIV IN THE LGBTQ+ COMMUNITY

THE HISTORY OF THE LGBTQ+ RIGHTS MOVEMENT™

# ACT UP!
## THE WAR AGAINST HIV IN THE LGBTQ+ COMMUNITY

RITA SANTOS

Rosen
YA
New York

*For CL and the New York Dancesafe Crew*

Published in 2019 by The Rosen Publishing Group, Inc.
29 East 21st Street, New York, NY 10010

**Expert reviewer**: Joey Lopez, director of outreach and health services, Ali Forney Center

**Library of Congress Cataloging-in-Publication Data**

Names: Santos, Rita, 1985– author.
Title: Act up! : the war against HIV in the LGBTQ+ community / Rita Santos.
Description: New York : Rosen Publishing, 2019. | Series: The history of the LGBTQ+ rights movement | Includes bibliographical references and index. | Audience: Grades 7–12.
Identifiers: LCCN 2017018718 | ISBN 9781538381243 (library bound) | 9781508183068 (pbk.)
Subjects: LCSH: AIDS (Disease)—United States—Prevention—Juvenile literature. | AIDS (Disease)—Political aspects—United States—Juvenile literature. | AIDS (Disease)—Patients—United States—Juvenile literature. | AIDS activists—United States—Juvenile literature. | Gays—Political activity—United States—Juvenile literature.
Classification: LCC RA643.83 .S26 2018 | DDC 362.19697/92—dc23
LC record available at https://lccn.loc.gov/2017018718

*Manufactured in the United States of America*

**On the cover:** Advocates for AIDS and HIV research like these marchers in a June 1983 Gay Pride parade (*top*) helped pave the way for lifesaving antiretroviral drugs like Truvada (*bottom*).

# CONTENTS

# INTRODUCTION

**W**hen people think of plagues, they tend to imagine a time much more primitive than our own, before the discovery of vaccines or antibiotics. However, in the 1980s, a plague came to the United States in the form of a little-understood virus, one that would later come to be named the human immunodeficiency virus (HIV). This virus specifically targets the immune system, the system in our bodies that protects against disease. Specifically, HIV attacks a part of the immune system known as CD4 cells (or T cells). As the virus destroys more and more T cells, it becomes harder for a person to fight off infection. When the immune system is so compromised that it can no longer fight off disease, HIV is considered to have progressed to a later stage known as acquired immune deficiency syndrome (AIDS). Once a person has AIDS, their life expectancy is generally no longer than three years. However, there is hope. Medical advances since the identification of HIV have prevented many cases from advancing to AIDS.

Scientists believe that HIV is a mutation of a virus found in chimpanzees in central Africa called the simian immunodeficiency virus (SIV). It is believed that hunters became exposed to chimpanzees' infected blood and that SIV later mutated into HIV.

As is often the case with viral infections, there are multiple strains of HIV. The two major types are HIV-1 and HIV-2. This history examines how HIV-1, henceforth called simply HIV, spread as well as the destruction it left behind.

Since the outset of the AIDS pandemic, those affected by it—such as these marchers in the 1983 San Francisco Gay Pride Parade—had to fight for recognition, respect, and adequate medical care.

The earliest documented case of an HIV infection was that of a man in Kinshasa, now the capital of the Democratic Republic of the Congo, in 1959. The virus spread from the Congo to other areas of Africa, eventually reaching the United States and other Western nations. That being said, HIV's long incubation period meant that many of those infected with the virus in the earliest years of its outbreak would not show any symptoms until the early 1980s. This would be the start of the AIDS pandemic.

AIDS is a devastating disease, but a combination of a slow response from the US government, poor funding, and prejudice against the most affected populations turned what could have been a small tragedy into a widespread crisis. One major factor in society's lulled response to the outbreak of HIV/AIDS is that the primary affected populations in its earliest years were members of the LGBTQ+ community. A combination of apathy and prejudice turned AIDS into a pandemic. Millions died because of those who refused to help or acknowledge the scope of the problem.

A look at primary and secondary historical sources tells the tale of how the HIV/AIDS epidemic unfolded. The minutes from government meetings, reports from the Centers for Disease Control and Preventions (CDC) and the World Health Organization (WHO), and interviews with HIV-positive patients and activists give the most accurate information to one studying these events. Activists were careful to document the crisis and research the effects of new medicines and courses of treatment. Although HIV/AIDS was a horrific tragedy for the LGBTQ+ community, from it rose one of the most accomplished and effective civil rights movements in US history.

# CHAPTER ONE

# A NEW CONSERVATIVE AGENDA

• • • • • • • • • • • • • • • • • • • • • • • • • • • • • • • • • • • • • • • • • •

After the growth of the gay rights movement in the 1960s, the LGBTQ+ community had been making slow progress toward civil rights. However, that progress would come to a halt with the election of Republican presidential candidate Ronald Reagan in 1980. Segments of his party held very conservative social views, including intolerance toward sexual minorities. Gay rights activists knew their communities would have a hard time after Reagan's victory. No one could have predicted the AIDS epidemic, though. The intolerance and indifference that came from the government in the wake of this outbreak needlessly allowed things to become much worse than they needed to.

## THE HEROIN EPIDEMIC

A decade before the AIDS crisis plagued the United States, the nation was dealing with an epidemic of a different kind. Between 1969 and 1974, the National Institute on Drug Abuse estimated a rise in the number of heroin addicts from 242,000 to 558,000. In 1986, the *New York Times* estimated that there were 500,000 heroin addicts in the

One common way HIV is transmitted is by sharing a needle with an infected person. Today, programs that exchange intravenous drug users' used needles for clean ones help prevent the spread of HIV and other diseases.

United States, with two hundred thousand of them in New York City.

Many states attempted to discourage heroin  use by passing laws making it illegal to own drug paraphernalia. These are objects used primarily for drug use. This law made it more difficult to acquire needles to inject heroin, causing drug users to often share the few needles they had. Sharing unsterilized needles was a perfect way to spread all kinds of infections. Doctors had already seen an epidemic of hepatitis B in injection drug users (IDUs).

As researchers from the CDC began to investigate what was killing gay men in the 1980s, they found that IDUs were also suffering similar ailments. Even though most heroin addicts told researchers they were not gay, the researchers initially assumed the men simply did not want to admit to taking part in a stigmatized lifestyle. As a consequence, medical institutions failed to see the link between the common ailments disproportionately affecting heterosexual IDUs and gay men.

Ronald Reagan formally accepts the nomination to become the Republican candidate in the 1984 presidential election in Dallas, Texas.

The life expectancy of heroin addicts with pneumocystis pneumonia (PCP) or Kaposi's sarcoma (KS) was significantly shorter than that of gay men. Thus, even if doctors wanted to study addicts with this illness, they probably wouldn't survive long enough for the doctors to make any meaningful discoveries.

## IN REAGAN'S AMERICA

To many, the election of former actor and California governor Ronald Reagan signified a return to more traditional American values. The religious right, a political movement that consisted of Christians who did not believe in the sepa-

ration of church and state, helped propel Reagan
to power. They wanted the morals of their religion
to dictate government policy. These values tended
to favor the lives and wants of straight, white, male
Christians over any other group. Reagan's victory
meant strong opposition to any measure that sought
to protect or give sexual minorities civil rights.

Many Americans believed people could simply
decide not to be gay. Those on the religious right
saw same-sex attraction and acting on those feel-
ings as an abomination. Considered a sin, same-
sex attraction went against the religious beliefs
of many. Some even considered homosexuality
to be a contagious disease, fearing that it could
spread to children. These beliefs led to discrimination in areas like employment and housing and
even pushed people to commit violence. Many
non-heteronormative people often didn't feel it was
safe to tell others in their community about their
sexuality, so they remained in the closet.

But social conservatism wasn't all Reagan offered
to voters. He also campaigned on a platform of lowering taxes and cutting government spending to stim-
ulate the economy. These money-saving tactics are
called austerity measures. The Americans who saw
tax cuts were generally wealthy and could afford to pay
more taxes. Similarly, cutting government spending
meant cutting back on services that were aimed at
helping the most vulnerable Americans. One of the
many government agencies that faced the harsh reali-
ties of spending cuts in 1981 was the CDC.

Although Reagan, the face of America at the time, disapproved of those who challenged heterosexual norms, the people of America—in some places more than others—were slowly learning more about their LGBTQ+ neighbors and, in turn, beginning to respect them. Certain cities, like San Francisco and New York, offered the LGBTQ+ community a safe haven, where they could live somewhat openly without fear of discrimination. Outside of these more tolerant areas, the rest of the country did not offer such acceptance. LGBTQ+ people often had to navigate one of two worlds, depending on where they were: one that was relatively accepting or one that was clearly intolerant.

Activists knew the fight for civil rights would be long, but many were basking in the tolerance they received in cities like New York and San Francisco, where they could openly find romantic partners and date in ways that were completely unavailable to people like them in the rest of the country.

## AN OUTBREAK

The heterosexual community experienced a sexual revolution spurred by the birth control pill. Although the LGBTQ+ community has little fear of unwanted pregnancy, they experienced their own sexual revolution. Since they could not legally marry, ideas about abstaining from sex until marriage were irrelevant. Many LGBTQ+ people engaged in unprotected sex and had active sex lives with multiple partners.

Suddenly, in 1980, gay men started to become sick. Doctors in New York and San Francisco noticed a handful of patients, all young men who were otherwise healthy, coming down with Kaposi's sarcoma (KS). This purple lesion-causing cancer had previously been seen in elderly men only. It was particularly notable how sick it seemed to make the young men. Usually, KS was not fatal and was easily treated.

Along with skin cancer, some young men also came down with pneumocystis carinii pneumonia (PCP), a severe lung infection caused by a small parasite. While it is likely that most people have been infected by this parasite, the majority don't get sick. These young men, however, were dying— and dying fast.

Doctors had never seen so many patients fighting multiple diagnoses. Diseases that their immune systems normally would have suppressed were overcoming their bodies' efforts to suppress them. Doctors refer to the array of illnesses these patients came down with as opportunistic infections, or illnesses that could only take advantage of an immune system that had been weakened.

## THEY CALLED IT GAY PNEUMONIA

Although most doctors have encountered illnesses they can't diagnose, it took just five patients with similar health issues for immunologist Michael Gottlieb and general practitioner Joel Weisman to notice that they were dealing with an outbreak. The CDC published a report Gottlieb wrote on the initial findings on those five patients. Soon, Gottlieb

## BABIES IN THE BRONX

In the early 1980s, Dr. Arye Rubinstein, an immunologist who specialized in pediatrics, noticed more and more infants coming in with mysterious immune system issues. His office was located in the Bronx, a borough of New York City with a lot of poverty. The parents of many of Rubinstein's patients were either injection drug users or had partners who were. He noticed that some of the mothers were also showing signs of immunodeficiency that matched those of the gay men he had heard of who were getting sick, but other doctors ignored this trend. Rubinstein diagnosed his patients with the same disease that gay men were getting, but other doctors would remove the diagnosis from the children's charts. Clearly, they thought, babies couldn't get a gay disease. The articles Rubinstein submitted to medical journals about his patients would be rejected on similar grounds.

Dr. Michael Gottlieb was a prominent early AIDS researcher. In late 1980, he began to work with patients exhibiting symptoms of the disease that came to be known as AIDS.

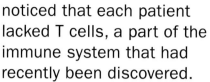

noticed that each patient lacked T cells, a part of the immune system that had recently been discovered.

When doctors research a new disease, they must uncover the similarities between infected people. Finding these similarities is important when it comes to determining if people are being made sick by something in their environment or from something like a virus. One of the few circumstances each patient shared was sexuality. All the men Gottlieb and Weisman treated were homosexual, a term often used pejoratively at this time by people who were hostile to gay people. Initially, the doctors thought that a bad batch of an illegal drug popular in some segments of the gay community called poppers could be the cause. If the cause was an infectious disease, the doctors knew it could signal the start of a public health crisis. The rate at which people were being diagnosed and dying from this mysterious illness revealed that this wasn't a contained crisis. Doctors soon realized that time was not on their side.

As a select few in the medical community began trying to spread the word about a new disease initially referred to as gay pneumonia or gay cancer, they ran into problems at every turn. The first problem was the lack of answers and explanations doctors had about the condition. No one knew how to alert the public about the disease without causing panic or more discrimination. How could they warn people about a possible infection if they didn't know how it spread?

As the CDC began to look into the disease, researchers learned that the Reagan administration budget cuts meant there was almost no money with which to do the research. The health of the LGBTQ+ community was not a major priority for medical professionals or politicians at the time, so gaining financial support would happen at an infuriatingly slow pace.

# CHAPTER TWO

# THE SEARCH FOR ANSWERS

● ● ● ● ● ● ● ● ● ● ● ● ● ● ● ● ● ● ● ● ● ● ● ● ● ● ● ● ● ● ● ● ● ● ●

E arly AIDS researchers faced every disadvantage imaginable. They were understaffed and under-funded. Their patients were some of the least cared about members of society. Patients didn't have years to wait for a slow scientific research process. Researchers looking into possible environmental causes of AIDS had to come up with theories based on a lifestyle they were unfamiliar with. For some medical professionals, their ingrained intolerance made gathering field research harder. Some CDC staffers, for example, were hesitant to go into places like gay bars or clubs because of the social stigma.

What follows are the stories of those who were dedicated to figuring this disease out once and for all.

## THEORIES ABOUND

Early researchers were desperate to uncover not only what was making their patients ill, but also what was infecting them. What was it about the

This 1985 photo of the Castro Bean depicts one of San Francisco's most prominent gay neighborhoods. The AIDS epidemic hit the Castro District particularly hard.

sexual activity of gay men that was causing their immune systems to fail? At first, doctors considered the theory that a bad batch of drugs was the cause. However, clusters of the same illnesses in patients who had been sexually involved with each other pointed to a sexually transmitted infection (STI).

Because many of the early victims of the epidemic had more than one STI, some doctors believed that the number of diseases the men had was overloading their immune systems. The thinking was that these men had so many diseases at the same time that it had destroyed their immune systems. Other doctors believed that a mutation of viruses like feline leukemia or cytomegalovirus of the herpes family caused the illness. Still other doctors came up with different theories, like the idea that poppers had created cancer-causing semen in gay men.

As doctors raced to find a cause, they also knew that they needed to figure out the mode of transmission. There was no way to stop new infections until they knew exactly how the disease got into the body. Early on, some doctors feared that the disease spread through unprotected sexual activity, but the long incubation period of HIV made that hard to prove. It was difficult for scientists to prove that two men who engaged in sexual intercourse caused an illness. There were just too many other variables. One of the things doctors feared most was a disease that spread like hepatitis B, which was an STI that could be spread through blood. Such a disease

# DISEASE TRANSMISSION

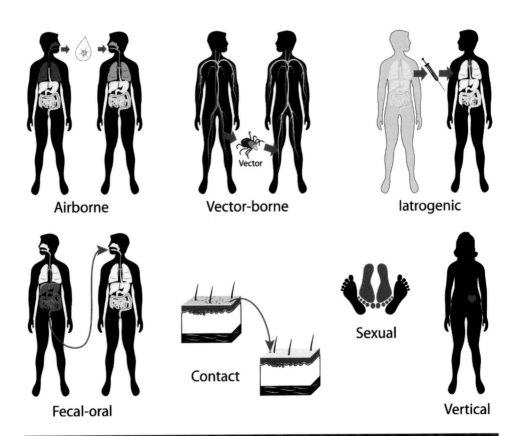

Airborne

Vector-borne

Iatrogenic

Fecal-oral

Contact

Sexual

Vertical

This diagram portrays seven ways that disease transmission can occur.

had the potential to spread far beyond the gay population of several major cities. Still, the medical community couldn't agree that a virus caused the disease, let alone that people could pass it on to one another.

## GRID

In 1982, the institutions working with infected men were more desperate than ever. Searching for something to call the cluster of diseases affecting gay men, the medical community declared this mysterious illness gay-related immune deficiency (GRID). CDC researchers immediately disliked the name and refused to use it. With no money to hire researchers, doctors working on the disease were left largely hoping for volunteers. But finding people who would work on a "gay disease" was nearly impossible.

The name had another unintended effect: it caused many doctors who were unfamiliar with the presentation of GRID to discount heterosexual patients. Injection drug users with the disease tended to die faster than patients who contracted the disease via sex. This meant that CDC researchers often weren't able to interview them before they passed away. Researchers were often told that these drug users actually had been gay; they just didn't want to admit to something that was considered taboo. When the children of drug users also showed signs of being infected with GRID, most doctors refused to believe that an infant could have a "gay disease." Early reports of women being infected were not initially released to the public.

The gay label caused doctors and researchers to turn a blind eye to the fact that viruses infect bodies, not sexualities. In the early days of GRID, anyone presenting symptoms of the terrible disease who wasn't gay often wasn't diagnosed with GRID. Some doctors assumed that given the comparably small size of the gay community, the disease would run its course, and the epidemic would end. However, other doctors realized that it was only a matter of time before GRID spread beyond the gay community. Some knew that it already had.

## HEMOPHILIACS

With no blood test for GRID, there was no way to determine if the national blood supply was infected. Doctors feared the possibility that the country's blood supply could be infected, for if it was, GRID now had a new way of spreading.

Blood banks, worried about what a tainted blood supply would mean for profits, decided to ignore initial warnings from researchers. All doctors could do was wait, knowing that anyone who received a blood transfusion could be at risk. Researchers who theorized that GRID could be transmitted through blood transfusions suspected that people with hemophilia, a genetic disorder characterized by a missing or defective blood-clotting protein, would be the next group to present symptoms, since they often require blood transfusions as part of their treatment regimen.

They were right. In July 1982, the CDC reported that three hemophiliac men from different areas (Westchester County, New York; Denver, Colorado; and northeastern Ohio) all contracted PCP, one of the signature ailments of GRID. The hemophiliac community was hesitant to be linked to a "gay disease" and did their best to avoid the social stigma associated with gay people.

Hemophiliac specialists were also wary of warning patients that a blood product called factor VIII could be a cause of infection because it was such a necessary treatment for hemophilia. Without factor VIII, the life expectancy of hemophiliacs dropped by nearly forty years.

Blood banks were slow to take action when hemophiliacs became infected because they feared a loss of revenue. They didn't want to spend money on interviewing blood donors about their health or on screening blood for a virus they weren't convinced existed. An accurate blood test to screen for HIV would not be invented until 1985. By that time, an estimated 40 percent of the American hemophiliac population had been infected with the disease. It's estimated that more than four thousand, out of ten thousand, American hemophiliacs died of HIV/AIDS.

## THE FOUR H'S RECEIVE MEDICAL NEGLECT

By the end of 1982, there were four clearly defined high-risk groups for contracting GRID. Researchers

# HOSPITAL VISITATION RIGHTS

Hospitalization is hard on all families. For the partners of some LGBTQ+ people, there are extra hurdles. In 2010 President Barack Obama issued a memorandum concerning the rights of hospital patients to choose and receive visitors and to designate a surrogate decision maker. Up until then, it was common for hospitals to deny visiting rights to same-sex couples. Hospitals regularly denied men who wanted to visit dying lovers and friends during the AIDS epidemic. This cruel practice isolated patients from their loved ones and prevented advocacy for proper treatment. Although Congress made no law protecting visitation rights for same-sex couples, many hospitals wrote new rules about patient visits that reflected the many different varieties of families that existed.

This 1990 photo portrays a man visiting his dying partner at the Maitri Zen Hospice in San Francisco.

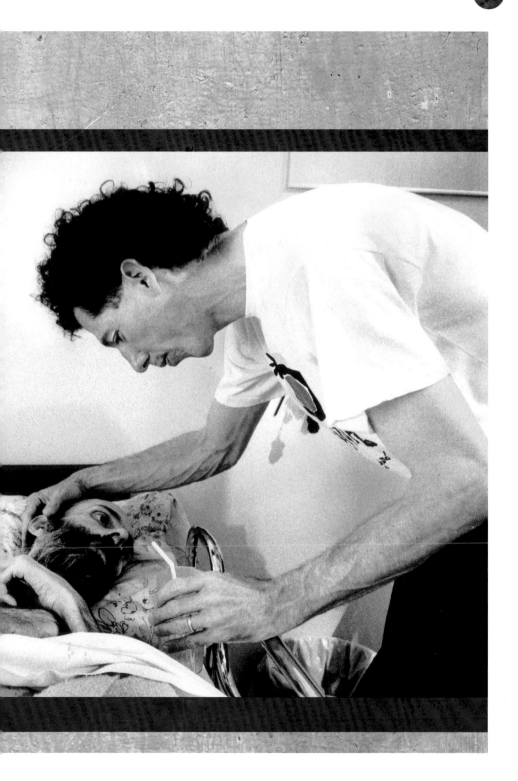

knew them as the Four H Club: homosexuals, heroin addicts, hemophiliacs, and Haitians.

Because the spread of GRID was similar to that of hepatitis B, doctors knew that gay people, injection drug users, and hemophiliacs were all at risk. The outbreak in a group of recent Haitian immigrants was a surprise.

There was much to hinder studying the Haitian patients. Researchers didn't have the money to study yet another population that was so little cared about by American society at large. Many of the immigrants had come to the United States illegally or had friends and family who had. This situation made them wary of speaking to government officials from the CDC. They feared deportation and other negative reactions from the US government, so they didn't cooperate with researchers. Even when researchers could find Haitian patients who were willing to answer questions, language barriers would hinder the CDC researchers. Consequently, in-depth research into the cause of GRID in the Haitian immigrant population was largely abandoned.

Health care workers knew that just like with hepatitis B, it was only a matter of time before they became the fifth H in the growing epidemic.

Although doctors who watched their patients wither and die in a matter of months understood that time was of the essence, larger institutions did not. It took years for researchers to receive grant money and what money they did receive was nowhere near enough. Doctors attempting to

In Miami, Florida, there is a large Haitian immigrant population in an area known as Little Haiti. This 1986 photo portrays some Haitian immigrants celebrating in the streets.

publish reports in medical journals meant to warn other doctors of the disease were told they had to wait the standard six months for publication. And these were the conditions given to the few who were not rejected by a publication. When reports were accepted for publication, the doctors weren't allowed to discuss their findings until after the papers were published. Because most diseases take years to become fatal, medical journals didn't understand the need to publish as soon as possible. Part of the lack of urgency also came from an overall apathy toward the gay community.

# CHAPTER THREE

# AIDS AND THE FIGHT AGAINST STIGMA

T o admit that you were sick with GRID meant not only confessing to being infected with a life-threatening illness, but also coming out of the closet. Many gay men either weren't ready to discuss their sexuality or didn't feel safe doing it. Homosexual acts were still a crime in many localities. It was legal to deny gay people housing and jobs. The stigma that surrounded GRID's association with the gay community severely limited even what researchers could do. As the 1980s progressed, doctors found themselves fighting social stigma alongside the effort to determine what, exactly, was wrong with their patients.

## THE FIRST CONGRESSIONAL PROBE

The opening statement of Representative Henry Waxman (D-CA) at the first congressional probe into the GRID epidemic in April 1982 echoed what most of the gay community was thinking:

*This horrible disease afflicts members of one of the nation's most stigmatized and discriminated against minorities. The victims are not typical Main Street Americans. They are gays ... There is no doubt in my mind that if the same disease appeared among Americans of Norwegian descent, or among tennis players rather than gay males, the response of both the government and the medical community would have been different.*

Waxman had a large LGBTQ+ population in his congressional base in Los Angeles. He understood how important it was for the government to take the epidemic seriously. Waxman would remain a congressional champion for the disease for the length of his forty-year political career.

By the end of the probe, the National Cancer Institute (NCI) had offered to release $1 million for KS research. Those familiar with the size of grants the NCI usually gave out knew the sum wasn't even 1 percent of the usual grants that the institution awarded. Similarly, while the Reagan administration had technically increased the CDC's budget by $5 million, none of that money was slated for GRID research.

In 1982, the National Institutes of Health (NIH) had spent $36,100 per death on toxic shock syndrome and $34,841 per death on Legionnaires' disease. But it had spent only $8,991 per death on GRID. Even worse was the fact that at the time, the combined death toll of toxic shock syndrome and

Representative Henry Waxman was one of the first government officials to call for funding AIDS research and prevention.

Legionnaires' was still less than that of the death toll of GRID. It would be another three years before the president would make even a passing public reference to the epidemic.

## A DIFFERENT NAME FOR THE SAME DISEASE

It wasn't just politicians who didn't want anything to do with the GRID epidemic, even though it had spread to almost half of the country. Many in the medical field had their own prejudice to deal with. And with so little funding going to GRID, many doctors simply saw no future in researching a disease that so few cared about, even though GRID was something totally unlike anything the medical world had ever seen before. Its association with gay men stopped researchers in their tracks.

While doctors simply chose not to research GRID, things were getting darker in hospitals. Some nurses who were scared that they'd become infected had begun to refuse to treat GRID patients. Many nurses weren't willing to be placed at high risk of contracting a disease that was 100 percent fatal. Those nurses, as well as some others in the medical profession, thought it was best not to take any chances. As the epidemic grew, so too would this line of thinking until AIDS patients would be completely shunned by society.

With the addition of hemophiliacs and Haitians to the list of at-risk communities, it was clear that GRID was no longer simply "gay related."

Researchers from the CDC had never liked the name GRID, and doctors knew the stigma associated with it was hurting their patients. Members of the gay community and the medical community were frustrated with the media's silence surrounding the disease. The media weren't interested in running stories about sick gay people. Only a handful of news articles had been published even though the epidemic was a year old and showed no sign of slowing down. In fact, GRID got the most press when heterosexuals began to be diagnosed with it.

In the summer of 1982, it was decided that the disease formerly known as GRID would now be called acquired immune deficiency syndrome (AIDS). The name didn't single out any one group of patients. The word "acquired" implied the disease was caused by something outside the patient's body, rather than something like a genetic disease. To many, dissociating the disease from its primary victim seemed like the only way to get desperately needed attention.

The name change was a necessary step, but the damage of GRID had already been done. Although the public still knew very little about the epidemic, what they did know was that it was something gay men got.

## IT'S IN THE BLOOD

With infections appearing in hemophiliacs and several people who had received blood transfusions,

# TIMOTHY WESTMORELAND AND BILL KRAUS

Although the executive branch of the White House was perfectly fine with ignoring the AIDS epidemic, two openly gay men in the legislative branch weren't. Bill Kraus started out as a gay rights street activist working with Harvey Milk, the first openly gay elected official in California. He stayed in politics after Milk's assassination in 1978 by becoming an aide to Congressman Philip Burton. Timothy Westmoreland was Congressman Henry Waxman's aide. He had helped orchestrate the congressional probe into GRID. What little money Congress did direct through legislation toward the AIDS epidemic came from the efforts of these two men.

Kraus died of complications due to AIDS in 1986. Westmoreland continued working to get funding and health insurance for people with AIDS throughout his career. When asked about how the epidemic changed his work as a health care advocate, he said:

> AIDS has also dramatized the gap between the middle class and the poor in this country. Access to health care really is a question of life or death. And disposable income is key; cash makes a difference between people living or dying.

Harvey Milk (*left*) speaks to lesbian feminist activist Gwenn Craig and Bill Kraus. Kraus was greatly influenced by his time working for Milk.

researchers at the CDC feared that AIDS had infected the nation's blood supply. However, the Food and Drug Administration (FDA), which had the power to regulate blood banks, thought the CDC was grouping unrelated diseases together under one name to receive more federal funding. They refused to put out regulations for a disease they weren't convinced was real.

Blood banks that could have instituted their own regulations had a hard time figuring out how to handle the epidemic. Many called for a ban on gay donors. Others feared a ban would stigmatize them even more. Self-reporting seemed like a good compromise, but the long incubation period of AIDS meant that people who seemed perfectly healthy could be carrying the disease unknowingly. Another issue with self-reporting was that some gay men who had trouble finding work because of discrimination would supplement their incomes at blood banks that paid donors. These men weren't likely to disclose their sexuality if it meant losing the money they desperately needed.

Blood banks were also extremely concerned with the costs of screening. They would lose a lot of money if they had to start interviewing donors and examining blood for a disease that doctors still had no test for. The closest thing to an AIDS test doctors could come up with was to search for hepatitis B, a disease that almost all AIDS patients had as well. But even that wouldn't catch all the infected blood. Added to that was the fear that a lack of donors would cause a blood shortage, a medical crisis in its own right. In

The Food and Drug Administration is responsible for making sure new drugs are safe and effective before they're administered to the public. The FDA's headquarters is located in White Oak, Maryland.

1982, it was a certainty that AIDS was in the blood supply. It would take almost a year after this discovery for the FDA to finally issue regulations.

The FDA banned all men who had sex with men from donating blood in 1983. In 2015, this lifetime ban was revised: men who had not had sex with men in the past twelve months would be allowed to give blood.

# PATIENT ZERO

As doctors tried to prove that the epidemic was in fact a sexually transmitted disease, they began to create patient webs to try to connect as many of the patients as possible. During the extensive interviews the CDC conducted, one name came up over and over again: Gaëtan Dugas. He would soon become known as patient zero.

Dugas was a Canadian flight attendant. Because of his employee discount, he was able to fly to San Francisco and New York regularly. Dugas had had more than one thousand sexual partners. In a 1984 paper prepared by the CDC, forty cases of AIDS all over the United States led back to Dugas. These webs were anonymous, with each man being identified by a number rather than his name, to protect the identities. However, because Dugas was from Canada, he was assigned the letter O. O stood for "Out of California." The O was widely misread by many as a zero. This misinterpretation, along with the fact that Dugas had had more than one thousand sexual partners, led many to believe that he was the person who had brought AIDS to the United States.

Although Dugas was among the earliest infected in the late 1970s and although he did pass the disease on to many people, he did not bring the disease to the United States. In 2016, researchers

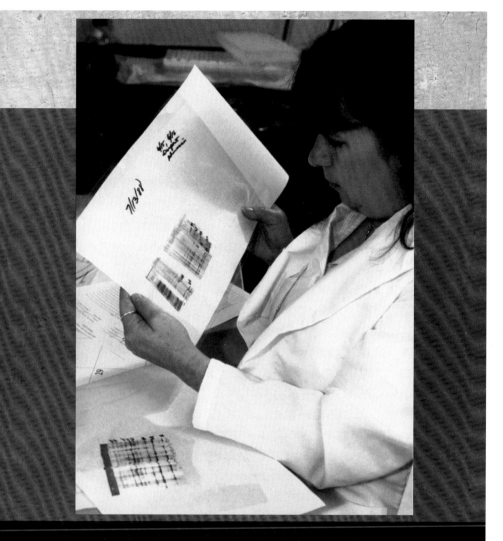

In 1984 the CDC traced forty US cases of AIDS back to "patient zero." Continued investigations eventually confirmed that AIDS came to the United States through Haiti in 1969.

who traced the origin of AIDS were able to demonstrate that AIDS entered the United States through Haiti in 1969.

## SILENCE EQUALS DEATH

As doctors searched for answers in laboratories across the United States, gay men were looking for answers as well. Doctors theorized that the disease was spread through bodily fluids, but without a test for the disease, they couldn't even be sure which bodily fluids spread it. Without proof of their theories, most health organizations felt uncomfortable releasing official guidelines about how anyone could lower their risk of infection. They wanted to avoid causing public panic.

LGBTQ+ rights activists battled over whether or not to tell people to limit their sexual activity. Their fear was that if they equated the illness with homosexual acts, it would only further stigmatize them. And with no official statements about the disease from health organizations, the LGBTQ+ community had only rumors to inform their understanding of the crisis. Was it poppers causing the disease, as they'd heard months ago? Was it, as many believed, a government conspiracy to kill off the gay population? Was it all a hoax being spread by bigots wanting to scare gay men straight? No one seemed to know what was happening, and the government wasn't talking. The newspapers weren't talking. A lot of gay men were sick and a lot of them were dead and no one in power seemed to have anything to say about it.

Despite growing evidence that AIDS was being spread through sexual contact and blood products, the groups involved in the fight against the epidemic were hesitant to openly promote abstinence of any kind. Some in the medical community and in the LGBTQ+ community thought places like gay bathhouses, where men often met for anonymous sex, should be temporarily shut down as a public health hazard. Others feared that the closure of gay businesses would lead to the loss of other civil rights that past LGBTQ+ rights organizers had given their lives to secure. In the fight against AIDS, there would be no easy answers.

# CHAPTER FOUR

# DEALING WITH IT ALONE

· · · · · · · · · · · · · · · · · · · · · · · · · · · · · · · · · · · · · · · · · · · · · ·

The AIDS epidemic only made the discrimination the LGBTQ+ community faced more apparent. It provided people with yet another reason to look down on anyone who deviated from the status quo, and, at this time, homosexuals fit the bill perfectly. Although the government preferred to keep quiet about AIDS, private citizens did not. The Christian ministers who were part of the religious right argued that the disease was "God's punishment for homosexuality." Some government officials did choose to speak out on the issue. Pat Buchanan, the communications director for President Reagan, referred to AIDS as "nature's revenge on gay men." As the epidemic grew beyond the LGBTQ+ community, however, so did the general public's fear of contracting the disease.

Members of the gay communities in New York and San Francisco realized they needed help that the government simply refused to provide. They soon came to face a harsh, but all too true reality: the gay community would receive no aid.

# ORGANIZATIONS ADVOCATE FOR THE SICK

On August 11, 1981, a group of men met in author Larry Kramer's apartment in New York City. They gathered to hear Dr. Alvin Friedman-Kien speak about the "gay cancer." After hearing more about the disease that was killing so many people they knew and cared for, the group raised $6,600 that they planned to donate to medical researchers. Just five months later, on January 4, 1982, six of the men in that original group, including Larry Kramer, met again, ready to do more. They intended to begin with raising funds for research and care, but they soon realized that people needed much more. By the end of that meeting, their mission stretched wider than anyone could have imagined, and they founded the world's first AIDS-advocacy organization, the Gay Men's Health Crisis (GMHC).

They started with a hotline offering what little information they had. It received a hundred calls the first day. Because the people calling needed more than just information, GMHC began to put together the Patient Services Division. That division provided social services that the city refused to offer to people with AIDS. GMHC also started a buddy program to fight social isolation and help those who were sick and had no one around to help them. These buddies would do everything from take people to the doctor to perform household tasks for the person they were assisting when they were too weak to do so. GMHC was run and operated entirely by volunteers. While the LGBTQ+ and AIDS community still had a long way to go, the creation of this organization was a flicker of light in the darkness, a sign that people were, in fact, capable of coming together in a time of crisis.

Only four months later, a group of men in San Francisco set up the Karposi's Sarcoma Research and Education Foundation, later renamed the San Francisco AIDS Foundation, in a small office on Castro Street. According to Cleve Jones, one of its cofounders, the phone started to ring as soon as it was turned on and it has been ringing ever since. Just like GMHC, the goal of the San Francisco AIDS Foundation was to get the most up-to-date information out to the community. A step ahead of the medical community, the members of this foundation stood in the streets, telling men to practice safe sex to anyone who would listen.

## ACT UP!

By 1983, Larry Kramer's blunt style had caused the GMHC and Kramer to part ways. Kramer's departure from the group didn't mean he was done being loud. He had always favored using direct action and civil disobedience tactics to get attention. Knowing that it would be harder for the government to remain silent if activists were regularly in the news, he formed the group known as AIDS Coalition to Unleash Power (ACT UP).

Playwright Larry Kramer was one of the first HIV/AIDS activists. He was a primary force behind the Gay Men's Health Crisis and ACT UP.

The group's first action was a march on Wall Street in New York City to demand better access to experimental AIDS medication. Many of the members of ACT UP belonged to the theater industry. As such, they understood how important it was for their dramatic style of protest to have a clear message, often one that told a narrative.

Some saw the group's actions, like their Stop the Church protest on December 10, 1989, in Saint Patrick's Cathedral in New York, as disrespectful. The protest was in response to the Roman Catholic Church's prolife stance and their disdain for AIDS education and the distribution of condoms. During the protest, ACT UP members entered the church during Mass, throwing condoms and lying down in the aisles. These activists thought the church's position against safe-sex education in schools and its view of people who partook in gay sex was equally disrespectful and deadly. While many were horrified by the protest, it proved to be effective in that it brought attention to ACT UP and changed many people's views of the Catholic Church. The insitution had previously been seen by some as untouchable, but not anymore. On September 14, 1989, ACT UP members chained themselves to the VIP balcony of the New York Stock Exchange to protest pharmaceutical company Burroughs Wellcome setting a $10,000 yearly price tag on the lifesaving AIDS medicine AZT. Days later, the company dropped the price to $6,400.

While ACT UP can be credited with many victories, there was one that completely changed the

ACT UP activists are seen here holding a die-in at the Food and Drug Administration to call for the end of double-blind medical trials for terminal diseases.

medical world as far as AIDS was concerned: the ending of double-blind medical testing for terminal diseases. Usually, when a new drug was being tested, one patient would be given the drug and another would be given a placebo, and neither the doctor nor the patient would know who had gotten which pill. Although these kinds of studies are often the best way to go about medical testing, the quick progression of AIDS meant placebo patients in the double-blind study would die before being treated with lifesaving medicine.

## THE AIDS QUILT

Harvey Milk was a politician in San Francisco and the first openly gay elected official in California. He was assassinated in 1978. Every year since his death, his good friend and fellow activist Cleve Jones organized a march in his honor. When it was time to plan the 1985 march, nearly everyone Jones knew was dead, dying, or caring for someone dying of AIDS. He learned that more than one thousand of his neighbors had died of the disease. He realized, "There was no way to adequately memorialize their death, and no place where we could gather to collectively mourn." Jones knew that that year's march needed to change that. He asked marchers to bring cards with the names of the loved ones they'd lost to AIDS. At the end of the march, they taped each name to the wall of the federal building. It reminded him of a patchwork quilt.

# DR. IRIS LONG

Iris Long was a retired pharmaceutical chemist from Queens, New York. In 1987, she attended an ACT UP meeting despite having no connection to the LGBTQ+ community. She just wanted to volunteer her time to help fight the epidemic ravaging the city she called home. With her background in chemistry and medical research, she was able to explain the complicated information about the types of drugs being used to treat HIV in terms everyone could understand. This clarification helped patients understand their treatment and health better. Her guidance also allowed the group to understand how to better target their demands and which protest causes were the most important and pressing. Her help raising awareness about treatment and clinical trials for HIV patients worked to save countless lives.

The sight would inspire the NAMES Project Foundation. Its goal was to create a quilt square to honor the death of every person with AIDS. Jones said he meant the quilt to be "A traditional American symbol of family and community, applied to *my*

The AIDS Quilt was laid out on the National Mall on October 11, 1996. It stretched from the Washington Monument to the US Capitol.

family and *my* community, to channel our love and grief and to break through the ignorance and prejudice that were stalling the nation's response to AIDS." The response to the project was huge. People from all over the country volunteered to help in its creation.

On October 11, 1987, the quilt was laid out for the first time on the National Mall in Washington, DC. The names of the dead covered more space than that of a football field. During the National March on Washington for Lesbian and Gay Rights, millions of people viewed the quilt. There were immediate requests from cities that had been hit particularly hard by the AIDS epidemic asking for NAMES to bring it to them, initiating what became a four-month tour of the quilt. In 1989, the world's largest community art project was nominated for a Nobel Peace Prize. The quilt project carries on in its quest to raise awareness about AIDS and AIDS prevention as it continues to tour. Unfortunately, the quilt continues to grow as more people die of the disease.

# CHAPTER FIVE

# CHANGING THE FACE OF AIDS

. . . . . . . . . . . . . . . . . . . . . . . . . . . . . . . . . . . . . .

As early as 1983, scientists knew how HIV was spread. However, getting that information out to the public was proving problematic. The first hurdle had been getting any news coverage at all. The second challenge came with the words reporters used to cover the disease. Although scientists knew the disease was only transmittable through blood and certain bodily fluids, including semen and vaginal fluids. Reporters were wary of using words like "semen," for fear that it would offend their audience. It was seen as impolite for adults to reference sexual acts or use proper biological names. Reporters used euphemisms instead, usually saying "bodily fluids" rather than "semen" or "blood." However, this usage caused undue confusion and panic in the general public who were left to wonder if "bodily fluids" also meant saliva and sweat. Could a clammy handshake lead to infection? This kind of misinformation led to people like Ryan White being both feared and bullied. In the media's attempt to avoid panic and offense, they created a climate of confusion and fear around AIDS that only helped the disease spread more.

## RYAN WHITE'S STORY

When Ryan White was just three days old, he was diagnosed with a severe form of hemophilia that required him to have weekly blood transfusions. Even with his condition, Ryan was a normal kid growing up in Kokomo, Indiana. In 1984, though, his doctors realized the pneumonia the middle

Ryan White (*left*) surrounded by friends at his new high school, Hamilton Heights in Arcadia, Indiana. Ryan's struggle with his old school earned him notoriety as the "new face of AIDS."

schooler was battling was really HIV. His mother was told that he would live only another three to six months, but, to everyone's surprise, by 1985, White was doing much better.

White wanted to go back to school because he missed his friends. Luckily for him, his doctor cleared him to return. However, the parents of his classmates weren't pleased with the decision. They'd knew little about HIV and even less about how it was transmitted. Parents feared White could infect their children. Even though doctors assured the school and parents that White could not infect other students just by going to school with them, almost half of the parents of his middle school and even some teachers signed a petition asking the school to ban him. The school refused to readmit White, so his mother took legal action and won the right for him to return to school.

When White was allowed to return to school, many parents took their children out. As a result, White had few friends. The school, which still didn't understand that he wasn't a risk, wouldn't allow him to use the restroom with other students and forced him to use disposable utensils at lunch. White's belongings were often vandalized with antigay slurs. The family eventually moved after someone opened fire on their home.

After his experiences in middle school, White was understandably nervous to start high school. He was happy to learn that, prior to his enrollment, the students of his new high school had been educated about AIDS. These students weren't afraid to shake his hand.

# NO INNOCENT VICTIMS

As news of White's legal battle with the school and the harassment he and his family faced spread, the public perception of AIDS began to change. Those who were infected through blood transfusions were now seen as "innocent victims" by the public. While Christian political pundits continued to proclaim that AIDS was a punishment from God, White pushed back. In an interview with the *New York Times* after his death, his mother, Jeanne, said, "Ryan always said, 'I'm just like everyone else with AIDS, no matter how I got it.' And he would never have lived as long as he did without the gay community."

Although White wanted to be a typical kid, he felt a responsibility to speak up for others with AIDS. He participated in numerous charity events for children with AIDS and took every chance he could to educate people about his disease. The media attention also garnered him some celebrity friends like Elton John, who became a close family friend. In spite of his doctor's initial prediction that White would live only six months, he surpassed all expectations and lived another five years after his diagnosis. He died on April 8, 1990, only a month before graduating from high school.

After his death, Congress enacted the Ryan White CARE Act, which is the largest federally funded program for people with HIV/AIDS. The program is meant to help low-income patients receive the care and medical attention they require.

White's activism helped chip away at the discrimination that surrounded AIDS. He showed the American people that diseases didn't target certain groups, nor were they punishments from God. The media that covered his struggle also highlighted the president's silence on the epidemic that was infecting more and more Americans every day.

## THE PRESIDENT BREAKS HIS SILENCE

On May 31, 1987, President Reagan finally addressed the nation about the epidemic that was in its sixth year. His friend and fellow movie star Elizabeth Taylor had become a staunch AIDS activist. The charity she and several prominent AIDS doctors had founded, known as the American Foundation for AIDS Research (amfAR), was holding a fundraiser, and it was there that President Reagan made his first official remark about the epidemic.

President Reagan's speech mentioned injection drug users and hemophiliacs but completely neglected to mention the impact of HIV and AIDS

on the LGBTQ+ community. He offered little fac-
tual information about what the disease was or
how Americans could prevent infection. In terms of

In this 1987 photo, philanthropist Joan Kroc (*left*) donates a million
dollars to the American Foundation for AIDS Research, the organization
founded by actress Elizabeth Taylor (*right*).

containing the disease, Reagan's speech offered no more than a dream that was impossible to achieve. But with the federal government no longer able to ignore the epidemic, things slowly began to change.

## THE WATKINS COMMISSION

Once President Reagan could no longer continue to overlook the epidemic, he organized the President's Commission on the HIV Epidemic. It was the commission's job to study the epidemic and advise the administration on the best way to combat it. Reagan asked Dr. Eugene Mayberry, the CEO of the Mayo Clinic, who had no experience with the disease, to lead the task force. The only person he appointed to the commission who had any real experience with AIDS was the openly gay geneticist Frank Lilly, a man who sat on the board of the Gay Men's Health Crisis. After Mayberry stepped down, Reagan tapped James D. Watkins, a US Navy admiral, to lead the council.

To the surprise of many, under Watkins's guidance, the commission was able to put together a comprehensive report that recommended close to five hundred steps the US government could take in combating AIDS. One of the most important recommendations the commission made was to create a federal antidiscrimination law for people with AIDS. Watkins understood that people feared the discrimination Ryan White and the gay community faced and, as a result, avoided being

# ROCK HUDSON

Rock Hudson was a famous movie star in the 1950s and 1960s who had been good friends with President Reagan from the time they were young actors together. Hudson had stayed at the White House several times.

Although most of his peers in Hollywood knew that Hudson was gay, he kept it hidden from the public. It was the only way for him to continue working in Hollywood. That is why, in 1985, the world was shocked to learn that Hudson had passed away of complications due to AIDS.

The media coverage of his illness and sexuality was largely sympathetic. It forced many Americans to reevaluate their views on homosexuality and AIDS. Hudson, like Ryan White, made AIDS victims more than a demographic discussed in newspapers. People began to realize that if someone as admirable and well known as Rock Hudson could die from AIDS, anyone could.

Hudson was aware of the impact his celebrity status brought to the perception of AIDS. Before his death, he said, "I am not happy that I am sick. I am not happy that I have AIDS. But if that is helping others, I can at least know that my own misfortune has had some positive worth."

tested or treated. The commission explained that the stigma of AIDS needed to be lifted to effectively combat the disease.

As the commission suggested, the Reagan administration worked to inform those who had received infected blood transfusions of their risk, and it increased funding for the CDC and NIH to research the disease. However, the Reagan administration refused to enact any antidiscrimination laws and ignored many of the other steps the commission outlined to get a handle on the epidemic.

## THE SURGEON GENERAL ACTS

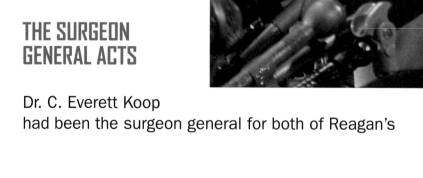

Dr. C. Everett Koop had been the surgeon general for both of Reagan's

Admiral James Watkins, chairman of the President's Commission on the HIV Epidemic, urged President Reagan to declare AIDS a public health emergency.

presidential terms. At the start of the AIDS epidemic, he repeatedly attempted to get permission to address the disease; and yet, every time, he was denied for reasons that were never fully explained to him. A large part of Koop's agenda was to remove the moral arguments that hindered the response to the epidemic. He stated, "My position on AIDS was dictated by scientific integrity and Christian compassion…. My whole career has been dedicated to prolonging lives, especially the lives of people who were weak and powerless, the disenfranchised who needed an advocate: newborns who needed surgery, handicapped children, unborn children, people with AIDS."

Koop, who had been forced to remain silent during the first four years of the epidemic, had a better understanding than most of just how deadly mixing religious arguments with medicine was to the sick and to people who refused to understand the problem. In 1988,

Surgeon General C. Everett Koop holds a news conference to announce that the government will mail every American household a pamphlet with information about HIV/AIDS.

Koop was finally allowed to mail brochures of information about HIV/AIDS and the best preventative measures to take to every home in America. It was a step most European nations had taken several years earlier. Conservative groups criticized the brochure for advocating safe sex rather than abstinence and for mentioning oral and anal sex. Some LGBTQ+ rights groups felt that the brochure's focus on anal sex in a way that described it as higher risk sex would cause more discrimination. Despite the criticism he faced from the public and the roadblocks put in place by the executive branch, Koop fought hard to get necessary information to the American people. He encouraged schools to begin sex education classes that included information about safe sex for students in grades three and up. Koop understood that without a vaccine the only way to prevent new infections was to educate the nation.

# CHAPTER SIX

# EDUCATION AND MEDICATION

● ● ● ● ● ● ● ● ● ● ● ● ● ● ● ● ● ● ● ● ● ● ● ● ● ● ● ● ● ● ● ● ● ● ● ● ● ● ● ●

O ne of the most controversial ways the surgeon general and AIDS activists went about fighting the epidemic in the last half of the eighties was to advocate for harm reduction. Conservatives tried to teach people that they had two options: abstinence from sex and abstinence from drugs. By contrast, other people realized that these were not realistic goals and used harm-reduction methods to educate the public. Harm-reduction practices are based on the idea that if you can't stop people from engaging in risky behavior, you can at least give them tools to make that behavior slightly safer.

## NEEDLE EXCHANGE IN NEW YORK CITY

In 1987, Mayor Edward Koch of New York City started the first needle-exchange program. Even though New York had the most AIDS cases of any city in the United States, the mayor had largely ignored the epidemic. Many speculated that his inaction was because he did not want to be associated with the LGBTQ+ community. But with the Reagan administration finally acting, others had to as well.

Needle-exchange programs create places where injection drug users can turn in their used needles for clean ones and sometimes be given a safe place to inject. Advocates knew addicts would continue to share needles if they didn't have ready access to clean ones, so they thought programs like these would curb the rates of new infections in injection drug users. Critics of the program thought that giving people access to clean needles would encourage drug use among children.

Even though the needle-exchange program was successful in lowering the rate of new

Needle-exchange programs often grappled with hostile laws that encouraged an all-or-nothing system. Under such laws, complete abstinence from drugs was the only acceptable way to avoid infection.

infections, the program was made illegal shortly after Koch left office.

In 1990, members of ACT UP started an underground needle-exchange program of their own. It was located on the Lower East Side of Manhattan. Their plan was to challenge the law by breaking it, thus forcing a court case. Intentionally breaking the law is part of a tactic activists use called direct action. Eventually, after studies showed that needle-exchange programs didn't cause drug use to rise, the laws were changed in 1992, and the exchange programs were brought back.

## HARM REDUCTION IN SEXUAL EDUCATION

In an announcement that the *New York Times* called "unusually explicit," the surgeon general made an impassioned plea for early comprehensive sex education in schools. In 1986, Koop wrote a report that outlined the type of education needed to help prevent the spread of HIV/AIDS. In the report, the surgeon general wrote,

> *Many people, especially our youth, are not receiving information that is vital to their future health and well-being because of our reticence in dealing with the subjects of sex, sexual practices and homosexuality. This silence must end. We can no longer afford to sidestep frank, open discussions about sexual practices—homosexual and heterosexual.*

*Education about AIDS should start at an early age so that children can grow up knowing the behaviors to avoid to protect themselves from exposure to the AIDS virus.*

Koop did state repeatedly that abstinence and monogamy were the best ways to protect oneself from infection. He also understood that these goals were not realistic for many. Members of the religious right, however, strongly believed that children should be taught only according to Christian morals when it came to sex education. They believed that even the discussion of sex would cause a rise in teen sexual activity. Beginning in the Reagan administration, the government began funding sex education that advocated only for abstinence, even though this went directly against the surgeon general's recommendations. Later, in the 2000s, President George W. Bush significantly increased spending on these programs.

Abstinence-only sex education often received the criticism that it promoted the spread of misinformation to students. A 2011 study found these programs to be misleading students about the effectiveness of condoms and birth control. They also left out potentially lifesaving medical information.

## A NEW DRUG

As researchers began to receive more funding, they started testing medications that already

# AIDS IN POP CULTURE

As AIDS reached pandemic levels around the world, artists began to react in the way they knew best—through their art. During the late 1980s and early 1990s, many artists used their crafts to tackle the epidemic. Larry Kramer, who was a novelist and playwright before becoming an AIDS activist, wrote the play *The Normal Heart* in 1985. The play is a mostly autobiographical account of Kramer's experiences becoming an AIDS activist.

Keith Haring was a popular painter and sculptor in the 1980s. Many of his paintings touched upon themes of frustration, fear, and isolation that were common in artistic portrayals of the epidemic. Haring lost his life to AIDS-related complications on February 16, 1990.

Perhaps one of the most famous pieces of art to come from the AIDS epidemic is the musical *Rent* by Jonathan Larson. The musical is a somewhat glamorized portrayal of life in New York's economically distressed Lower East Side. The majority of characters in the musical are HIV positive or have AIDS. The play was praised for its uplifting and positive portrayals of queer characters and people with AIDS. Larson died of an aortic dissection on the morning before *Rent*'s first Broadway preview performance. The show went on to win the Pulitzer Prize for Drama and three Tony Awards, while the song "Season of Love" became a pop hit that is often played at graduation ceremonies. *Rent* gained a cult following and became one of the longest-running shows on Broadway.

*Rent* is not the only well-known theatrical work to address HIV/AIDS. Tony Kushner (*left*) wrote *Angels in America*, a play about people from all walks of life coping with the AIDS crisis. A huge success, it won two Tony Awards and a Pulitzer Prize for Drama.

existed to see if anything would have an effect on the virus. In March 1987, the FDA announced the approval of an antiretroviral drug called Zidovudine (AZT) as a treatment for HIV/AIDS. The drug was originally intended to fight cancer, but it had failed at that purpose. It did, however, prevent HIV cells from spreading. Unfortunately, doctors at the time didn't know that long-term AZT use is toxic because it also causes healthy cells to stop replicating. Many patients felt worse from the side effects of AZT than before they were treated.

It turned out that the initial dosages of AZT that were prescribed to patients were much too high. The severity of the side effects was partially caused by the high doses. The dosages also caused patients to develop drug resistance sooner. When doctors realized their mistake, they lowered the doses and patients responded better. AZT was by no means a perfect drug, but it was the only drug available then. In 1987, AZT treatment usually added about a year to the life of a person with AIDS, but patients would take as much time as they could get.

## LAZARUS EFFECT

As scientists continued searching for a cure, they finally reached a major medical breakthrough in 1996. Doctors combined several types of antiretroviral drugs into what would colloquially become known as the AIDS cocktail. The medical names for the treatments were highly active antiretroviral therapy

# MAGIC JOHNSON

Earvin "Magic" Johnson Jr. was an incredibly popular basketball player for the Los Angeles Lakers. He had a promising career ahead of him when he stunned the nation by announcing that he was HIV positive and would be retiring from basketball. He contracted the disease by having un-protected heterosexual sex.

Even though he had retired, he was still chosen to play for the United States in the 1992 Olympics. He did play, and he led his team to winning the gold medal.

Johnson became an AIDS activist after his retirement. He hoped to help educate others about the disease. His openness about his illness helped to dispel some of the stigma surrounding the disease. The straight ballplayer used his influence to show that AIDS could affect anyone, no matter their sexuality.

Earvin Magic Johnson Jr. is awarded a gold medal as a member of the US men's basketball team at the 1992 Olympics. His announcement that he was HIV positive helped fight the stigma against HIV.

(HAART), combination antiretroviral therapy (cART), or antiretroviral therapy (ART). Each of these names stand for the same thing, prescribing a patient a combination of drugs based on where the patient is in the virus's progression. The main goal of this treatment is to prevent the virus from becoming drug resistant while also lowering the patient's viral load, or the amount of the virus detectable in a patient's blood.

The AIDS cocktail consists of nucleoside reverse transcriptase inhibitors (NRTIs), non-nucleoside reverse transcriptase inhibitors (NNRTIs), and protease inhibitors (PIs). These all prevent HIV from replicating. There are two other drugs in the cocktail, and these prevent the virus from entering

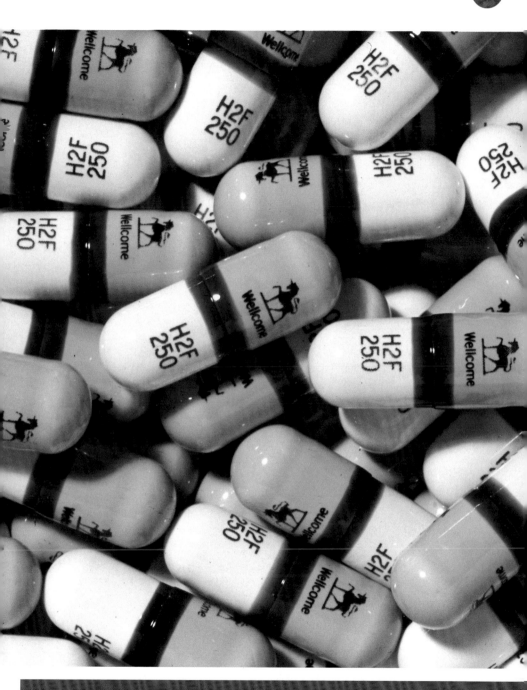

This 1985 photo shows AZT in capsule form. It was also made available in syrup form. Like many pharmaceutical drugs, AZT came with a plethora of side effects.

cells. They are known as entry/fusion inhibitors and integrase inhibitors.

Although the side effects of these drugs can be hard for patients to handle, 1996 was the year that AIDS went from being a fatal disease to a manageable chronic disease. The treatment worked so well that it was referred to as the Lazarus effect because patients who had previously been wasting away were now much healthier. AIDS was no longer a death sentence for many. In fact, for the first time, people could say they were "living with AIDS." But this wasn't true for everyone, AIDS medications were, and in some cases still are, prohibitively expensive. AIDS became a "disease of poverty" because only those who could afford treatment would survive.

# CHAPTER SEVEN

# THE FUTURE OF AIDS

• • • • • • • • • • • • • • • • • • • • • • • • • • • • • • • • • • • • • • •

D ecades of hard work have produced lifesaving medical breakthroughs in the fight against AIDS. People living with HIV/AIDS who are properly medicated now have life expectancies similar to those who are not infected with the disease. Many of the drugs that make up the AIDS cocktail have been combined so that patients can take one pill rather than several. And in 2002, the FDA approved the first rapid HIV diagnostic test. This test allowed patients to find out their HIV status in one visit to the doctor. Then, in 2004, the FDA approved an oral swab rapid HIV diagnostic test. Without a vaccine or cure, though, the only way to end the epidemic is to halt new infections.

## DREAMING OF A FUNCTIONAL CURE

AIDS researchers are working on two different types of cures. The first is called a functional cure, which means that HIV cells will be suppressed to the point that they are undetectable in the blood and the chance of transmitting the virus to others is greatly reduced. It's only a functional cure because the virus still lives within the body of the patient; it's just no longer making that person sick. Whereas some doctors think the AIDS cocktail is a functional cure, others believe that a functional cure will be reached when patients no longer need to take daily medication.

In 1998, the *New York Times* reported on a man of anonymous identity who accidentally and mysteriously achieved this functional cure. He is referred to as the original Berlin Patient and has remained anonymous. On May 10, 1996, he contracted HIV by having unprotected sex. Three weeks later, he was tested for HIV, and on June 20, the results came back positive.

After a few weeks of taking the antiviral medications called indinavir, didanosine (ddI), and hydroxyurea, he was hospitalized with a testicular infection. He had forgotten to bring his medications with him and during the days he spent in the hospital, the virus resurged. He left the hospital and went back on his medications for four months and found the medications to have successfully overtaken the virus.

However, an infection of hepatitis A caused him to stop taking his medicatic

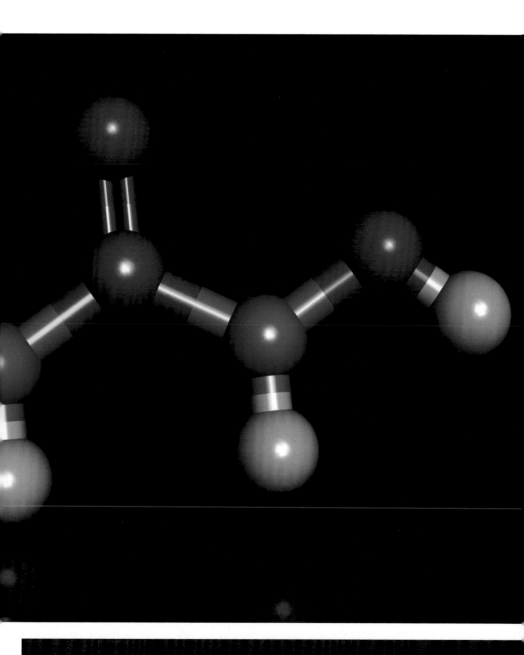

This model portrays a hydroxyurea molecule. Hydroxyurea is one of the drugs that may have contributed to the anonymous Berlin Patient's mysterious functional cure.

some reason, this time he didn't notice the reemergence of the symptoms that appeared the first time he stopped the medications. He felt it would be fine to never go back to them, despite his doctor's advice. He was lucky, too, because for some unexplained reason, the virus did not progress to full-blown AIDS.

Doctors have been unable to ascertain whether it was the specific medications he took, the unsteady exposure to the virus, or some natural immunity that kept his HIV from advancing to AIDS. For this reason, science has not discovered a clear path of medical therapy that can replicate such a favorable outcome as a functional cure in other patients. It is thus still the recommended practice for doctors to prescribe continuing antiretroviral therapy without interruption.

## THE BERLIN PATIENT 2.0: AN ELUSIVE STERILIZING CURE

The second type of cure AIDS researchers are working on is called a sterilizing cure. This type of cure would completely kill the virus. According to *Plus*, a publication about HIV, scientists have so far achieved this result in a second person, who also became known as the Berlin Patient.

Timothy Ray Brown of Seattle, Washington, was diagnosed with HIV in 1995 while he was studying in Berlin, Germany. For many years, he took antiretroviral medications to keep the disease at bay. In 2008, Brown faced another medical crisis, a form of blood cancer called leukemia. After receiving a bone marrow transplant from a donor

This picture shows a happy and healthy Timothy Ray Brown at the 2012 International Symposium on HIV and Emerging Infectious Diseases assembly.

who had a mutation in their CCR5 gene that made that person immune to HIV, doctors could find no trace of HIV anywhere in his body even though he was no longer taking antiretroviral medication.

Brown also suffered from graft-versus-host disease, a complication from bone marrow transplants in which the donor's white blood cells attack the patient's healthy cells. Doctors think the disease may have played a part in curing Brown's HIV. As recently as May 2017, it has been reported that a handful of people with both cancer and HIV have undergone bone marrow transplants that resulted in the same short-term results. *New Scientist* described the situation as such: "Only one of the six received bone marrow from a person with the CCR5 mutation—however, all six developed graft-versus-host disease." Only time will tell if these patients will be cured of HIV the way Brown was, but if anything is clear, it's that our understanding of HIV/AIDS and possible treatments continues to grow.

## A RECENT OUTBREAK IN THE UNITED STATES

In December 2015, Indiana had what a CDC director called "one of the worst documented outbreaks of HIV among IV users in the past two decades," according to *USA Today*. Two rural towns faced the same issues that New York City had in the 1970s: an economic depression, an injection drug epidemic, and a ban on needles.

# HOW TO REDUCE YOUR RISK OF HIV INFECTION

Knowing one's own HIV status as well as the status of any sexual partners is the first step to reducing one's risk of being infected. It's important to get tested regularly.

Reducing one's exposure to semen, vaginal fluids, breast milk, and blood during sexual or other contact is also important. Physical barriers like male and female condoms are one means of reducing exposure while still allowing for sexual contact. These are ways to practice safe sex. Not sharing or using unsterile needles during injection drug use is another means of reducing exposure to HIV. In general, alcohol and drug use may lower one's inhibitions so that a person is less discerning, which can lead to unsafe sexual practices. Many medical care providers, reproductive health clinics, and public health clinics offer free condoms and syringe- or needle-exchange programs.

In 2014, the CDC introduced a preventive regimen called preexposure prophylaxis (PrEP), which can help individuals reduce their risk of contracting HIV. The only drug currently approved for this regimen is called Truvada. PrEP is recommended for people who are at high risk of exposure on a regular basis, such as injection drug users, HIV-negative partners of HIV-positive people, or members of populations with disproportionately high rates of HIV infection (such as men who have sex with men, African Americans, and Latinos). It is a daily medication intended for use

*(continued on the next page)*

(continued from the previous page)

alongside other harm-reduction methods such as using condoms. When taken appropriately, PrEP is highly effective at preventing HIV transmission.

Similarly, postexposure prophylaxis (PEP) is a treatment regimen of drugs meant to keep HIV from replicating after a person has already been potentially exposed to the virus. PEP is effective if the regimen is started within seventy-two hours of possible exposure to HIV. A doctor will prescribe the pills to be taken once or twice daily for a full twenty-eight days. Adherence to the regimen is necessary for the best shot at preventing the virus from replicating in a person's system. While PrEP is generally considered a better option for people whose routine behavior puts them at a higher risk for exposure to HIV, PEP is recommended for people who are not generally at risk of exposure and have possibly been exposed to HIV through an isolated unsafe encounter.

In extremely rare cases, people have contracted antiretroviral-resistant strains of HIV even while on PrEP. Furthermore, neither PrEP nor PEP prevent other STIs, and cost can be a prohibitive factor for low-income patients. Some critics of PrEP and PEP believe they undermine the value of condom usage and other safe-sex practices. However, when used properly and in combination with other safe-sex practices, PrEP and PEP are powerful tools to curtail the transmission of HIV.

In addition to tools such as PrEP and PEP, limiting one's number of sexual partners is a good sexual health practice, as is getting tested regularly, using condoms properly, and having frank conversations with sexual partners about their sexual practices and health.

This poster advertises PrEP as a pill that can prevent the spread of HIV.

Part of the problem stemmed from the fact that in 2011, the state government was run by religious conservatives who had voted to defund Planned Parenthood, a women's health organization, because of religious and moral objections. Planned Parenthood ran five health clinics in rural Indiana that were all shut down as a result of being defunded. They were the only places where the residents of the two towns could be tested, treated, or get information about HIV/AIDS.

Two months after the outbreak was declared, then-governor Mike Pence lifted the ban on needle possession. This action meant the towns could set up temporary needle exchanges, something Governor Pence was personally against. The needle exchanges, combined with the CDC's aggressive outreach, caused the number of new infections to drop. Contrary to Pence's expectations, this result demonstrated that harm-reduction efforts really do prevent the spread of disease.

## THE PRESENT AND THE FUTURE CRISIS

As of 2016, the pandemic that was recognized with just five sick patients in a few large US cities had killed approximately 675,000 Americans. As of 2017, 70 million people have been infected worldwide. A CDC report published in June 2015 stated that one in eight people living with AIDS in the United States is unaware of his or her status. In 2016, the CDC revealed that between 2005 and 2014, the rate of

# THE UNITED STATES HELPS COMBAT AIDS IN AFRICA

HIV originated in west-central Africa in the 1920s and spread rapidly throughout the continent. Many nations in Africa did not have modern health care systems that were capable of handling a disease epidemic of such magnitude. Africa would be the hardest-hit continent in the pandemic. As of 2015, 25.6 million of the 36 million people infected with HIV live in Africa.

President George W. Bush wanted to help combat the AIDS crisis since he first considered running for president. In 2002, Bush signed the President's Emergency Plan for AIDS Relief, or PEPFAR. It aimed to help African nations prevent and treat the disease.

In practice, PEPFAR has been criticized for spending funds on abstinence-only sex education in places like sub-Saharan Africa. Others believe that PEPFAR doesn't focus enough on harm-reduction and prevention techniques.

The abstinence-only aspect of the program failed to reduce the rate of infection. That being said, the program did help 7.7 million people with HIV receive antiretroviral medication and provided other services to those suffering from AIDS.

new HIV infections fell by 19 percent, but some demographics have seen their rates of infection rise. According to the CDC's New HIV Infections in the United States fact sheet, in 2010, African Americans accounted for 44 percent of new infections, while Hispanics accounted for 21 percent. AIDS.gov states that there are currently an estimated 36.7 million people living with HIV. Around 1 million people died of AIDS in 2016.

As the AIDS crisis began to become less of an urgent battle due to the medications that were discovered, many gay men who survived found their communities permanently altered. Gay men still account for 55 percent of all people currently living with AIDS. The death toll in the gay community was staggering, and many lost people they loved.

Before the crisis, few LGBTQ+ people had understood how important the demand for civil rights and political representation was. From hospitals and living rooms across the country, the LGBTQ+ community formed activist groups that

On World AIDS Day in 2006, hundreds of people gathered in the Washington, DC, Freedom Plaza for a candlelight vigil to remember those who have lost their lives to HIV/AIDS.

slowly grew more and more powerful as they needed the support of institutions that showed them nothing but hostility.

The fight for LGBTQ+ rights is far from over. In the majority of the United States, it is still legal to deny housing and employment to people based on their sexuality. This type of discrimination puts people at higher risk of poverty and health problems, like AIDS. Simiarly, the fight against AIDS still has a ways to go. Homophobia is still present in the medical community, and, as a result, people may be hesitant to seek preventatitve measures, treatment, or any other kind of help when they visit a doctor.

Although many factors contributed to the AIDS crisis, the biggest lesson to be learned from the American government's response to the AIDS crisis is the sad, but all too real, cost of intolerance.

AIDS has also taught Americans how much can happen when passionate people work together toward a common good.

Although rates of new infections are dropping, the recent outbreaks in Indiana prove that without vigilance, HIV/AIDS will remain a crisis. The need for harm reduction and comprehensive sex education continues to exist. For until there is a cure, it is only through the prevention of new infections that people can truly hope to end the epidemic. In 1988, Surgeon General Koop said, "Stopping AIDS is up to you," and it still is.

# TIMELINE

**1981** The CDC reports a cluster of pneumocystis pneumonia in five gay men in Los Angeles in the *Morbidity and Mortality Weekly Report*.

The term GRID is coined for the epidemic.

**1982** Gay Men's Health Crisis is formed to deal with the disease in New York City.

Congressman Henry Waxman organizes the first congressional probe into the epidemic.

AIDS is found in a baby who had received a blood transfusion.

The CDC renames GRID AIDS in the hopes of ending stigma surrounding the disease.

**1983** The CDC identifies all major routes of AIDS transmission.

The first dedicated outpatient center for AIDS patients opens in San Francisco.

**1984** Ryan White is diagnosed with AIDS.

**1985** The CDC puts out blood screening guidelines for all donated blood to protect the nation's blood supply.

Ryan White is banned from school because of his AIDS diagnosis. This event sparks nationwide debate.

Rock Hudson dies of AIDS-related complications.

**1987** The FDA approves AZT for treatment of HIV/AIDS.

President Reagan gives his first address dealing with the AIDS epidemic and announces the formation of the President's Commission on HIV.

The AIDS quilt is unfurled on the National Lawn.

**1988** Surgeon General Koop mails more than a million copies of the *Understanding AIDS* brochure to every household in America. It is the largest medical mailing in American history.

**1991** Magic Johnson announces he's HIV positive.

**1996** The AIDS cocktail antiretroviral drug therapy regimen becomes standard.

**2007** The Berlin Patient Timothy Ray Brown is cured of AIDS.

**2016** Governor Mike Pence declares a state of emergency in Indiana due to an HIV outbreak that occurred in December 2015.

# GLOSSARY

**acquired immune deficiency syndrome (AIDS)** The later stage of an HIV infection in which the immune system has been compromised and the infected person is susceptible to opportunistic infections.

**antiretroviral drugs** Drugs used to treat HIV without curing it that try to prevent the virus from spreading to cells that haven't been infected.

**Centers for Disease Control and Prevention (CDC)** A US government agency that tracks the evolution, cause, and means of transmission of diseases.

**direct action** Demonstrations such as strikes, blockades, boycotts, or picketing that attempt to achieve a desired societal or organizational change.

**drug resistance** When a virus or bacteria has mutated to the point that it is no longer affected by a medicine that was used to treat it.

**epidemic** An infection that spreads quickly to many people, animals, or plants.

**factor VIII** A protein that assists in the clotting of blood that can be used to treat hemophilia. Factor VIII that was donated from people with AIDS prior to screening practices passed the infection to the recipients.

**functional cure** A cure that suppresses a disease to the point where it is undetectable in the blood, does not progress, and the risk of transmitting it to others is greatly reduced.

**graft-versus-host disease** A disease that can

occur following a bone marrow or other form of tissue transplant in which the transplant's white blood cells reject the healthy cells in the recipient's body.

**harm reduction** Actions that allow for harmful behaviors but try to cushion the harm, like suggesting not sharing needles during drug use to prevent disease transmission.

**hemophilia** A genetic condition that limits the body's ability to clot blood following an injury that can easily lead to a person bleeding to death.

**human immunodeficiency virus (HIV)** A virus that infiltrates the immune system's helper T cells in order to replicate. The act of replication compromises a person's immune system and modifies DNA.

**immune system** The body system that fights off infection to maintain health.

**Kaposi's sarcoma (KS)** An opportunistic infection that is a skin cancer and a common complication of an HIV infection.

**National Institutes of Health (NIH)** A biomedical research facility that is a division of the United States Department of Health and Human Services.

**opportunistic infection** An infection that occurs when a body's weakened immune system cannot suppress it anymore.

**pandemic** A disease that occurs throughout an entire country or the whole world.

**pneumocystis pneumonia (PCP)** An opportunistic

pneumonia infection that affects people with compromised immune systems.

**poppers** A slang term for amyl nitrates, a recreational drug that was associated with the gay club scene.

**postexposure prophylaxis (PEP)** A treatment regimen of drugs meant to keep HIV cells from replicating after a person has been exposed to the virus.

**preexposure prophylaxis (PrEP)** A treatment regimen of drugs meant to prevent infection of HIV in people who are at substantial risk of exposure to the virus.

**sterilizing cure** A cure that completely kills a disease.

**zidovudine (AZT)** The first antiretroviral drug that effectively treated HIV.

# FOR MORE INFORMATION

The Ali Forney Center (AFC)
321 West 125th Street
New York, NY 10027
(212) 206-0574
Website: http://www.aliforneycenter.org
Facebook: @AliForney
Twitter: @AliForneyCenter
The AFC is the largest organization in the United
    States dedicated to providing resources, includ-
    ing housing, job preparedness, and health care
    services, for LGBTQ+ youth who are homeless.

Care
151 Ellis Street NE
Atlanta, GA 30303
(404) 681-2552
Website: http://www.care.org
Facebook: @carefans
Twitter: @care
Instagram: @careorg
Care works to end poverty and poverty-related
    issues like AIDS worldwide.

Elizabeth Glaser Pediatric AIDS Foundation
1140 Connecticut Avenue NW, Suite 200
Washington, DC 20036
(202) 296-9165
Website: http://www.pedaids.org
Facebook and Twitter: @EGPAF
Instagram: @egpaf

This foundation seeks to end pediatric AIDS cases around the world.

Head and Hands
5833 Sherbrooke Street W
Montreal, QC H4A 1X4
Canada
(514) 481-0277
Website: http://headandhands.ca
Facebook and Twitter: @headandhands
This Canadian organization offers health and legal services to Canadian youth. It also advocates for harm reduction.

HIVEqual
606 West Avenue, Suite 2B
Norwalk, CT 06850
(203) 939-9408
Website: http://www.hivequal.org
Facebook, Twitter, and Instagram: @hivequal
HIV Equal strives to provide the most up-to-date information about HIV/AIDS to the world.

The Quilt: The NAMES Project Foundation
117 Luckie Street NW
Atlanta, GA 30303
(404) 688-5552
Website: http://www.aidsquilt.org
Facebook: @AIDS-Memorial-Quilt
Twitter: @AIDSQuilt
The AIDS memorial quilt continues to grow and tour, offering educational services when the group

visits cities. It remains the largest piece of folk art in the country.

YouthCo
205-568 Seymour Street
Vancouver, BC V6B 3J5
Canada
(604) 688-1441
Website: http://www.youthco.org
Facebook: @youthcovancouver
Twitter: @YouthCO
Instagram: @youthco
This organization provides information about HIV/AIDS to Vancouver youth and assistance to them.

# FOR FURTHER READING

Ashton, Jean, and the New-York Historical Society. *AIDS in New York: The First Five Years*. New York, NY: New-York Historical Society in association with Scala Arts Publishers, 2015.

Berlatsky, Noah. *HIV/AIDS*. Detroit, MI: Greenhaven Press, 2012.

Crawford, Dorothy H. *Virus Hunt: The Search for the Origin of HIV*. Oxford, UK: Oxford University Press, 2015.

Downs, Jim. *Stand by Me: The Forgotten History of Gay Liberation*. New York, NY: Basic Books, 2016.

Fan, Hung, Ross F. Conner, and Luis P. Villarreal. *AIDS: Science and Society*. Burlington, MA: Jones & Bartlett Learning, 2014.

Halkitis, Perry N. *The AIDS Generation: Stories of Survival and Resilience*. Oxford, UK: Oxford University Press, 2014.

Hillman, Bruce J. *A Plague on All Our Houses: Medical Intrigue, Hollywood, and the Discovery of AIDS*. Lebanon, NH: University Press of New England, 2017.

Katz, Jonathan D., Rock Hushka, Bill Arning, Christopher Castiglia, Christopher Reed, Glen Helfand, Robb Hernandez, Joey Terrill, Theodore Kerr, Amy Sadao, Nelson Santos, Teresa Bramlette Reeves, David Román, Sarah Schulman, Sur Rodney, Stephanie A. Stebich, Tacoma Art Museum, Zuckerman Museum of Art, and the Bronx Museum of the Arts. *Art AIDS America*. Seattle, WA: Tacoma Art Museum in association with University of Washington Press, 2015.

Meruane, Lina, and Andrea Rosenberg. *Viral Voyages: Tracing AIDS in Latin America*. New York, NY: Palgrave Macmillan, 2014.

Organista, Kurt C. *HIV Prevention with Latinos: Theory, Research, and Practice*. Oxford, UK: Oxford University Press, 2012.

Strub, Sean O'Brien. *Body Counts: A Memoir of Politics, Sex, AIDS, and Survival*. New York, NY: Scribner, 2014.

Whyte, Susan Reynolds. *Second Chances: Surviving AIDS in Uganda*. Durham, NC: Duke University Press, 2014.

# BIBLIOGRAPHY

Green, Joshua. "The Heroic Story of How Congress First Confronted AIDS." *The Atlantic*, June 8, 2011. https://www.theatlantic.com/politics /archive/2011/06/the-heroic-story-of-how -congress-first-confronted-aids/240131.

Institute of Medicine, Committee to Study HIV Transmission Through Blood and Blood Products, Harold C. Sox Jr., Michael A. Stoto, and Lauren B. Leveton. *HIV and the Blood Supply: An Analysis of Crisis Decisionmaking*. Washington, DC: National Academies Press, 1995.

Kallen, Stuart A. *The Race to Discover the AIDS Virus: Luc Montagnier vs. Robert Gallo*. New York, NY: Twenty-First Century Books, 2012.

Koop, C. Everett. "The C. Everett Koop Papers: AIDS, the Surgeon General, and the Politics of Public Health." NIH U.S. National Library of Medicine. Retrieved March 3, 2017. https:// profiles.nlm.nih.gov/ps/retrieve/Narrative /QQ/p-nid/87.

Louie, Kelsey. "It's Been 35 Years Since Gay Men's Health Crisis Began in Larry Kramer's Living Room." *Advocate*, August 11, 2016. http:// www.advocate.com/commentary/2016/8/11 /its-been-35-years-gay-mens-health-crisis-began -larry-kramers-living-room.

Lower East Side Harm Reduction Center. "History." Retrieved February 25, 2017. http://www .leshrc.org/page/history.

Parvin, Landon. "President Reagan's amFAR Speech." *Frontline*, May 31, 1987. http://www .pbs.org/wgbh/pages/frontline/aids/docs /amfar.html.

Rudavsky, Shari. "CDC: Indiana Has 'One of the Worst' HIV Outbreaks." *USA Today*, April, 28, 2015. https://www.usatoday.com/story /news/nation/2015/04/28/indiana-hiv -outbreak/26498117.

Schulman, Sarah. "ACT UP Oral History Project: Interview of Larry Kramer." MIX—the New York Queer Experimental Film Festival, November 15, 2003. http://www.actuporalhistory.org /interviews/images/kramer.pdf.

Schumaker, Erin. "Mike Pence's Defining Moment as Governor? Enabling an HIV Outbreak." *Huffington Post*, October 6, 2016. http://www .huffingtonpost.com/entry/mike-pence-indiana -hiv_us_57f53b9be4b002a7312022ef.

Sharp, Paul M., and Beatrice H. Hahn. "Origins of HIV and the AIDS Pandemic." *Cold Spring Harbor Perspectives in Medicine*: 1.1 (2011): a006841. PMC. Web. April 7, 2017.

Shilts, Randy. *And the Band Played On: Politics, People, and the AIDS Epidemic*. New York, NY: Penguin Books, 1988.

Tanne, Janice Hopkins. "Fighting AIDS on the Front Lines Against the Plague." *New York*, January 11, 1987. http://nymag.com/health/features /49240.

Westmoreland, Timothy. "Henry Waxman, the Unsung Hero in the Fight Against AIDS." *Politico*, February 4, 2014. http://www.politico.com/magazine/story/2014/02/henry-waxman-aids-fight-103123?o=1.

White, Ryan, and Ann Marie Cunningham. *Ryan White: My Own Story*. New York, NY: Signet, 1991.

Wilson, Clare. "Immune War with Donor Cells After Transplant May Wipe Out HIV." *New Scientist*, May 6, 2017. https://www.newscientist.com/article/mg23431244-400-immune-war-with-donor-cells-after-transplant-may-wipe-out-hiv.

# INDEX

## A

abstinence, 44–45, 68, 69, 73
  sex education, 91
acquired immune deficiency
  syndrome (AIDS)
  advocacy organizations, 47,
    48, 60
  artists and, 74
  in blood supply, 37, 40–41
  changing the face of,
    56–68
  cocktail, 76, 78, 80, 81, 82
  definition of, 6
  discrimination around, 28,
    38, 60, 62, 94
  education about, 48, 58,
    59, 66, 68, 72–73, 90
  effect of the epidemic, 46
  fear of, 56–57
  fight against the stigma,
    33–45, 64
  the future of, 81–94
  hemophiliacs with, 27
  incubation period of, 40
  medication, 50, 52, 76, 78,
    80, 81, 82
  method of transmission,
    44–45, 56–57, 58, 88
  naming of, 37
  and President Reagan, 38,
    60, 62
  progression of, 6, 78, 84, 86

  public perception of, 59
  quilt, 52–53, 55
  researchers, 21, 33, 36,
    47, 81, 84
  shunning of those with, 36
  start of the pandemic, 8,
    9, 66
  statistics on, 90, 92
  test for, 40
  treatment for, 86
activists, 8, 9, 15, 38, 44,
  48, 50, 52, 60, 69, 72,
  74, 77, 92, 94
Africa
  efforts to combat AIDS in,
    91
  as source of AIDS virus, 6, 7
American Foundation for AIDS
  Research (amFAR), 60
antiretroviral drugs (ARVs),
  76, 78, 84, 86, 91
AZT, 50, 76

## B

Berlin Patient, 82
Berlin Patient 2.0, 84, 86
blood banks, 26, 27, 40
blood transfusions, 26, 37,
  40, 57, 59, 64
bodily fluids, 44, 56
Brown, Timothy Ray, 84, 86
Buchanan, Pat, 46
Bush, George W., 73, 91

## ABOUT THE AUTHOR

Rita Santos has written several titles for young adults and children. She has a masters of science in publishing from Pace University. She lives in New York City with her family, and she is passionate about activism and students' rights.

## ABOUT THE EXPERT READER

Joey Lopez is the director of outreach and health services for the Ali Forney Center. He is a lifelong New Yorker who has been living with HIV for over twenty years. He has been a member of both the New York City and New York State HIV Prevention planning groups. He has also served on the New York City mayor's HIV/AIDS Health and Human Services Planning Council, through which New York City allocates federal Ryan White HIV/AIDS Program funds to the HIV/AIDS community.

## PHOTO CREDITS

Cover (top) Barbara Alper/Archive Photos/Getty Images; cover (bottom) Justin Sullivan/Getty Images; pp. 6–7 esfera/Shutterstock.com; pp. 7 (inset), 12–13, 31, 64–65 Bettmann/Getty Images; pp. 10–11, 22, 35, 38–39, 51, 54, 60–61, 66–67, 75 © AP Images; Images; pp. 18–19 Gary Friedman/Los Angeles Times/Getty Images; p. 24 Designua/Shutterstock.com; pp. 28–29 © Waldemar Hauschild/SZ Photo/The Image Works; p. 41 Congressional Quarterly/CQ-Roll Call Group/Getty Images; p. 43 CDC; p. 49 New York Daily News Archive/Getty Images; p. 57 Taro Yamasaki/The LIFE Images Collection/Getty Images; pp. 70–71 Andrew Holbrooke/Corbis News/Getty Images; p. 77 Aris Messinis/AFP/Getty Images; pp. 78–79 Science & Society Picture Library/Getty Images; pp. 82–83 MediaForMedical/Universal Images Group/Getty Images; p. 85 Gerard Julien/AFP/Getty Images; p. 89 Directphoto/age fotostock/SuperStock; pp. 92–93 Chip Somodevilla/Getty Images.

Design and Layout: Michael Moy; Editor: Bernadette Davis; Photo Researcher: Cindy Reiman

# INVENTING THE
# VIDEO GAME

BY HEATHER ADAMSON

**The Child's World®**
childsworld.com

Published by The Child's World®
1980 Lookout Drive • Mankato, MN 56003-1705
800-599-READ • www.childsworld.com

Acknowledgments
The Child's World®: Mary Berendes, Publishing Director
Red Line Editorial: Design, editorial direction, and production
Photographs ©: Creatas Images/Thinkstock, cover, 1; Michael Reynolds/EPA/Corbis, 4; SK2/HS1 WENN Photos/Newscom, 7; Pablo Martinez Monsivais/AP Images, 8; Joi Ito CC2.0, 10; Digital Game Museum CC2.0, 13; Wahyu Ichwandardi/Getty Images, 14; Mark Wilson/Reuters/Corbis, 17; Kyodo/AP Images, 18; iStockphoto, 20

ISBN 9781634074629

LCCN 2015946287

Printed in the United States of America
Mankato, MN
December, 2015
PA02284

ABOUT THE AUTHOR

Heather Adamson has been writing nonfiction children's books for many years. She loves the chance to learn new things. When she is not writing, she likes to watch birds and watch movies. She lives in South Dakota with her husband, two sons, and her dog named Quincy.

# TABLE OF
# CONTENTS

# Chapter 1

# THE BROWN BOX

Sometimes an idea just won't go away. That's how it was for Ralph Baer, the father of video games. He knew in the 1940s that TVs could do more than broadcast shows.

Baer ran three radio repair shops in New York. He was just beginning to work with TVs when he went to fight in World War II (1939–1945). After the war, he went to Chicago to study to be a television engineer. He was one of the first people to graduate with that degree. At first, most of his work was building radars or time clocks. But he kept thinking about the TVs he built in school.

In 1955, Baer's idea came back again. He was working for a company that made TVs. He wondered if something could be added to the company's TVs to make them better than other TVs. Maybe they could include a game. He mentioned the idea to his boss. But the company said no. They could not imagine such a crazy thing.

◄ The original Brown Box and its two controllers

Baer kept working in electronics. In 1966, while he was waiting for a bus, his idea struck again. He realized there were already more than 50 million TV sets in the United States. What if he could build a computer that hooked up to any TV? Baer balanced a tiny notebook on his knee. He sketched his ideas until the bus came. The next day at work, Baer wrote four pages explaining his idea. He called his idea "TV games."[1]

Baer put together a team to build the TV games. The team worked in a top-secret area of a large company. It took the team a few years to make a good working model. It was difficult to create a simple game that would not cost too much. Finally, in 1968, they completed the prototype. It became known as the Brown Box. It did not have sound, and the graphics were very basic.

Small blips of light moved on the screen. One of the games was like Ping-Pong. Two rectangle shapes on the screen were the paddles. A small square blip was the ball. Players used control boxes with three dials. One dial moved the paddle up and down. The other dial moved it side to side. The third dial was used for putting spin on the ball. Players tried to hit the ball past each other. Baer later said, "The minute we played Ping-Pong, we knew we had a product."[2]

▲ Baer demonstrates the Ping-Pong game
on the Brown Box.

Now Baer had to sell the invention. He showed it to lots of

people in the TV industry. No one dared take a risk on something

so new. Finally, a company called Magnavox bought the Brown

Box in 1971.

Magnavox changed the design a bit. The company added

plastic clings with pictures of crowds or stadiums to stick to

the TV. Other board games, dice, and score pads were added to the package. Magnavox named it Odyssey and called it a "Home Entertainment System."[3] After a few preview tours, the product started selling in the fall of 1972. Baer's dream of a TV game was finally happening.

But Baer was not happy with Magnavox's choices. The price was too high. And Odyssey was available in only a few TV stores. In three years, it sold about 200,000 units. It was not the millions Baer had hoped. But his idea for TV games was not lost. Another young inventor would use America's love of arcades and the invention of the microchip to bring Baer's TV game idea to life again.

◀ Baer received the National Medal of Technology in 2006.

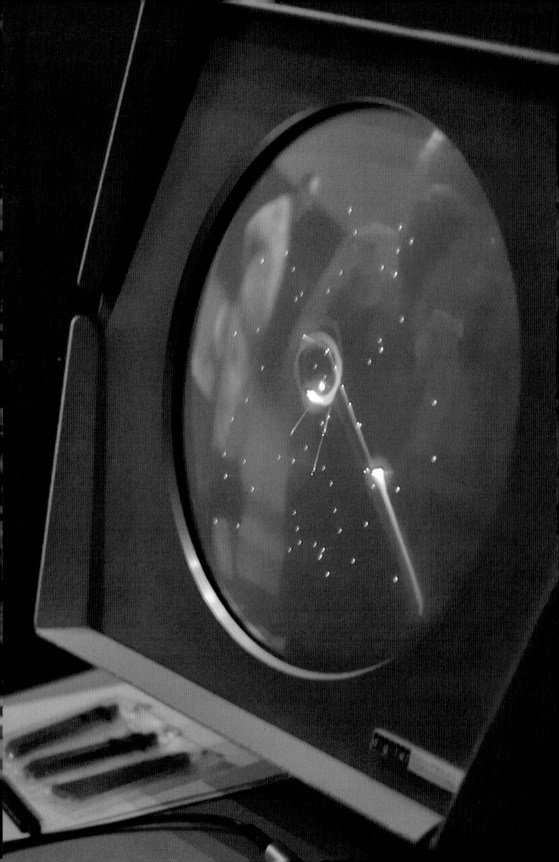

# Chapter 2

# NOLAN BUSHNELL'S IDEA

In the 1960s, Nolan Bushnell took a job at an amusement park to pay for college. He did not know that the job would change his life. In this work, Bushnell convinced people to pay 25 cents to throw balls at a stack of milk cans. He also tinkered with the pinball machines. And he fixed the motors that moved pictures behind the glass screens of carnival games. One day, Bushnell found out about a computer game at his college. He knew he had to play it!

In the 1960s, computers were massive. A single computer filled a whole room. Only a few places even had computers. Bushnell asked some friends to get him into the computer lab. There, he played a computer game called *Spacewar!* In the game, two fighting spaceships tried to avoid space dangers. Bushnell loved playing the game. It made him want to create games of his own. So, he learned to program computers. He wrote rows and rows

◀ *Spacewar!* **was created by computer scientist Steve Russell in 1962.**

of commands for the computer to follow. With his programs, he made a few simple games.

After college, Bushnell took a job as an engineer. But he did not enjoy it. He remembered how much he loved playing *Spacewar!* He decided to build a coin-operated computer game that was similar. A spaceship would fly around asteroids and fire at attacking ships. He tried creating the game for a new mini computer. But the processor was too slow. Changing out the parts would make the game cost too much. He would have to start from scratch.

Bushnell built a circuit board for the game. He bought a used TV for the screen. Then he used an empty paint can for the coin box. To cover his used parts, he built a fancy spaceship-like cabinet. The game was called *Computer Space*. It was a free-standing unit with a screen that players stood in front of.

Bushnell sold the prototype to a company that made games. About 1,500 *Computer Space* machines were produced in 1971. But the game did not sell well. It was too tricky for people who did not use computers.

In May 1972, Bushnell saw a special preview of Magnavox's new Odyssey system. It had simple games that were easy and fun to play. One game was called *Table Tennis*. Bushnell knew why

▲ *Pong* (left) and *Computer Space* (right) were two of the first arcade video games.

his game had failed. It was too hard. He decided to make an easy Ping-Pong game.

In June, Bushnell and his friend Ted Dabney started their own company. They called it Atari. Their Ping-Pong arcade game was called *Pong*, and it sold more than 8,000 units. Many of the machines made $200 a week in coins. But Atari was not done changing the video game business.

**13**

# Chapter 3

# GAMING WARS

*P*ong proved that arcade video games could make money. But other companies started taking apart Atari's games to see how they were made. Then they copied the games and sold similar versions. This meant Atari was not making as much money as before. So, Nolan Bushnell went to work on a home version of *Pong*.

Bushnell learned from the mistakes of Odyssey. The home version of *Pong* had color, sound, and sharp graphics. And the invention of microchips helped make the system affordable. In 1975, Bushnell made a deal with Sears, a big retail store. In a few months, Sears sold 150,000 home *Pong* games. People seemed to love TV games!

Bushnell started working on a system with changeable game cartridges. In 1977, Atari released the VCS, which later became known as the 2600. By 1980, Bushnell knew Atari needed a popular game to boost its home sales. So he decided to make a

◀ The Atari 2600 came with a game called *Combat.*

home version of a popular arcade video game. *Space Invaders* was already a huge hit in arcades in Japan. People played the game so much that it caused coin shortages. When Atari released a home version of *Space Invaders*, it sold more than one million copies.

People bought the Atari 2600 just to play *Space Invaders* at home. But the gaming war was heating up. Other companies were quick to make gaming machines, too. People were going crazy for all the new games. Companies started making them as fast as possible.

Store shelves were now full of video games. But many games were not high quality. People got tired of paying high prices for poor games. By 1983, it looked like the end of video games.

Many unsold video games from the early 1980s ▶ were thrown in landfills.

# Chapter 4

# NINTENDO TO THE RESCUE

In 1983, stores in the United States were trying to get rid of their video games. They were filling the shelves with other things. Arcades were closing. Many video-game makers quit the business. But in Japan, Hiroshi Yamauchi knew people would always love playing a good video game. He was the head of a company called Nintendo.

In 1980, Yamauchi knew he needed to sell games in the United States. He asked one of his employees if he thought he could design a hit game. Shigeru Miyamoto told his boss, "I'd love to!"[4] Miyamoto created one of the first video games with a story. A gorilla named Donkey Kong grabs a man's girlfriend, and the man must rescue her. *Donkey Kong* came out in 1981. It was an immediate arcade success. Yamauchi used that success to create a new gaming system. It was called the Family Computer.

◀ **A Nintendo employee displays the *Donkey Kong* game and the Family Computer.**

▲ **Many people consider _Super Mario Bros._ to be the best video game of all time.**

In 1983, the Family Computer sold millions of units in Japan. But U.S. stores did not want to end up with lots of unsold games again. Yamauchi had to convince U.S. stores that the Family Computer would be different. So he put a gold seal of approval on games that met the company's quality standards. The company also made a game called _Super Mario Bros._ It was extremely popular. The Family Computer finally came out in the United States in 1985. But it had a new name. It was called the Nintendo Entertainment System. The system went on to sell more than 60 million units worldwide.

Since then, video games have continued to gain popularity. And this popularity shows no sign of slowing down. Graphics and gaming systems continued to advance. By the mid-2010s, millions of people were playing on systems such as Wii U, PlayStation 4, and Xbox One.

What will the future of video games look like? Nobody is sure, but one thing is certain. Video games have come a long way since Ralph Baer's idea in 1966.

## VIDEO GAME TIMELINE

| | |
|---|---|
| **1966** | Ralph Baer sketches his ideas for "TV games" while waiting at a bus stop. |
| **1968** | Baer and his team create the Brown Box. |
| **1971** | Nolan Bushnell creates an arcade game called *Computer Space*. |
| **1972** | Odyssey, the first home entertainment system, begins selling. |
| **1972** | Bushnell and Ted Dabney start Atari; they create the arcade game *Pong*. |
| **1980** | Atari releases a home version of *Space Invaders*, the first home version of an arcade game. |
| **1986** | The Nintendo Entertainment System sells more than one million units in the United States. |

# GLOSSARY

**arcades (ar-KAYDZ):** Arcades are businesses that have games people can pay to play. In the 1980s, arcades charged 25 cents to play most video games.

**circuit board (SUR-kut BORD):** A circuit board is a piece of plastic that has electrical circuits, or small metal strips. Nolan Bushnell built the circuit board that controlled the video game he invented.

**microchip (MY-kro-chip):** A microchip is a thin piece of silicon that contains electronic circuits. The invention of the microchip helped video games become less expensive.

**processor (PRAH-ses-ur):** A processor is a computer program that puts another program in a form the computer can use. A fast processor is necessary for video games.

**program (PRO-gram):** Program means to write a set of instructions that control the way a computer works. Bushnell knew how to program computers, so he could create his own computer games.

**prototype (PRO-to-typ):** A prototype is the first version of an invention. Before selling a product, a company usually builds a prototype to make sure the product works.

# TO LEARN MORE

## Books

Cunningham, Kevin. *Video Games: From Concept to Consumer.* New York: Children's Press, 2014.

Jozefowicz, Chris. *Video Game Developer.* Pleasantville, NY: Gareth Stevens, 2010.

Powell, Marie. *Asking Questions about Video Games.* Ann Arbor, MI: Cherry Lake, 2015.

## Web Sites

Visit our Web site for links about video games: childsworld.com/links

*Note to Parents, Teachers, and Librarians: We routinely verify our Web links to make sure they are safe and active sites. So encourage your readers to check them out!*

# SOURCE NOTES

1. Ralph Baer. "Genesis: How the Home Video Games Industry Began." *Ralph H. Baer.* Ralph H. Baer, n.d. Web. 19 Aug. 2015.

2. "The Brown Box, 1967–68." *The National Museum of American History.* Smithsonian Institution, n.d. Web. 19 Aug. 2015.

3. Bill Loguidice and Matt Barton. *Vintage Game Consoles: An Inside Look at Apple, Atari, Commodore, Nintendo, and the Greatest Gaming Platforms of All Time.* New York: Focal Press, Taylor Francis Group, 2014. Print. xvii.

4. Van Burnham. *Supercade: A Visual History of the Videogame Age 1971–1984.* Cambridge, MA: MIT Press, 2003. Print. 247.

# INDEX